Dmitry Agarunov

I0481499

Sh!t
Happens

Insider's perspective on facing economic
and industry crises from
the founder of the world's largest
cybersecurity resource xakep.ru

Book edited by Artem Paschuk
pashchuk@glc.ru
Book designed by Lidiya Itina
itinall@gmail.com
Translated into English and edited by Sarah Crowther
sarah.r.crowther@gmail.com

2017

Preface

How would you characterize an event that results in losing your successful business, all your money, your health, your family, and still leaves you owing a million dollars? Although it happened to me when I was only thirty, I had acquired no lack of colorful expressions to describe my experience, the most innocent of which was "shit!"

That very first serious crisis to a large extent shaped my life as a businessman and a person. I have become resolutely determined that such "shit" should never happen again, and if it is impossible to avoid, I must be prepared and deal with it without such huge losses.

Continuing in business, I became convinced that crises happen again and again, whether I want them or not. They could be caused by external factors or my own managerial mistakes and miscalculations; they could affect the whole global economy, an individual country, one industry, or my company alone. All crises, regardless of their scale, reason, and circumstances, have enriched my experience as entrepreneur incredibly, for what I am grateful to them. However, now, fifteen years after my most hopeless "shit", I should admit that I have never developed an immunity to it – shit keeps happening to me and, in a sense, has become an inseparable part of the way I do business. Even now, working on this book, I am simultaneously reforming my company, terminating unprofitable projects, and exploring new growth points. The most important thing is that "shit" has stopped frightening me and ruining my life – I react to it in a calm and constructive way.

I know that I am not alone – many Russian entrepreneurs also do business in "S" mode, constantly switching from dealing with one problem that threatens to ruin their company to solving another one, no less painful. I don't think it prevents us from considering ourselves successful. After all, as Winston Churchill said, "Success consists of going from failure to failure without loss of enthusiasm." Challenges and failures help to keep us realistic, to retain our humility; they don't let us rest on our oars and lose our business acumen.

This book is not so much my biography, as a learning aid. Many of my own failures were caused by simple ignorance. There was no sage around to help me, who had already experienced my problems and knew how to overcome them. So, when I became convinced that the experience that I have accumulated could be useful to other entrepreneurs, I started sharing it immediately. Twelve years ago, I founded Svoy Biznes [One's Own Business] magazine, then became an active member of the global Entrepreneur's Organization (EO), and in recent years, I have become a regular speaker at business seminars and conferences. Now I have tried to summarize my experience in a book, which, I hope, will help others learn how to handle challenging situations in business and private life.

Chapter 1. The beginning.

The beginning and the middle of the 1990s in Russia were a time of emotional exhilaration in those who had entered the market economy. For most citizens of Russia, capitalism had not started up yet – people kept on working at large enterprises built during the times of the USSR; they were nostalgic about the past and didn't know how to deal with the new opportunities. In this dreary environment, I felt I was a part of the emerging merchant class and was proud of it. Oil then cost $12 per barrel and work in the oil and gas sector had not yet become prestigious. There were no large retail chains, so my chain of five retail outlets was already considered cool in its segment. I dreamt of building a nationwide network of video game stores, and felt I was part of the elite, the builder of a new reality.

The brilliance of the economic policy of the Yeltsin era was in the fact that the government completely removed itself from commerce. Taxes, customs, and regulation – nothing like that existed at all, and as a result, entrepreneurial activity boomed. The economy that fell into decay with collapse of the Soviet Union was rebuilt in the 1990s by hands of such petty entrepreneurs. They were not appreciated, nobody cared about them, but de facto we were then enjoying economic freedom. Freight was quickly delivered, there were no huge expenses for accountancy and paperwork, and the country was quickly flooded with goods, even with the low oil prices. To be fair, one should note that a different non-market factor was at play – gigantic IMF loans, which artificially supported the ruble exchange rate – but that doesn't belittle the contribution of millions of petty entrepreneurs, whose initiative promoted the recovery of trade, and which, in turn, affected the development of transport infrastructure, the commercial real estate market, etc.

One of the side effects of the state's self-removal from economy was the flourishing of crime. Famous "bratki" ["bros"], as mobsters were called in the 1990s, kept all businesses in fear, and I also had to play by their rules. They shared the profit in some of my stores, and handled all issues not only with the criminal world, but with the state too – I could be sure that I would not be visited by the authorities for any inspection that would result in me getting a summons or a fine. In other outlets, I was spared the necessity to directly contact racketeers, as their "services" were included in the rent: by renting a commercial space, I automatically hired a gang of "bros". Members of criminal groups accompanied my freight, working on the "everything included" principle. During this whole period, I had to deal with one or two "visits" from other gangsters, but I talked to my "consultants" and all questions ceased. I think one of the reasons that there were not many conflicts around my business was that we traded in video games. It was considered a "good" business that should not be pressed hard.

Conversely, bandits and policemen, who had no hi-tech toys as children, enjoyed their visits to our store to discuss the new releases of the gaming industry, ask for advice and buy something.

I have never been infatuated with the criminal lifestyle, thinking that bad police are better than good criminals. By definition, bandits can't work for the good of society, and the police, however corrupt they may be, will always include people who stand for law and order. When law enforcement authorities declared a war on crime and crushed most mob groups, it was both an unexpected and a happy piece of news.

Somewhere around 1997, my merchant dreams started to crumble. From an elite hobby, computer games turned into everybody's hobby, and this process was accompanied by the growth of pirating, while demand for original products remained low. But the rent for commercial property rose many times over. For instance, when I was opening an outlet of 12 square meters on Novy Arbat, I was paying $3,600 a month in rent, and when I was closing it, $24,000 a month! Yet the revenue, which at its peak had reached $150,000-200,000 a month, fell to $60,000. I had to close my stores at a loss. It was a shame, but the decline of one business was accompanied by flourishing of another: I started publishing a gamer's magazine, Strana Igr [Gameland], which instantly became a hit. Our portfolio also included the licensed Official Playstation Magazine. It didn't bring us any profit, but we felt great pride that Sony entrusted the issue of their official periodical to us, and nobody else! We thought our media business was prospering and intended to arrange for publication of several more magazines.

In the winter of 1998, I decided that my primary business would focus on media and not on distribution of video games and retail. At that moment, the circulation of Strana Igr had reached 80,000 copies and it was still growing; all copies were selling out. Now the video game trade started looking completely unprofitable. By July 1998, I only had a single store left, which remained profitable, but the earnings were several times lower than from the magazine, so my immediate plans also included closing the last outlet. I was not interested in spending my time and my effort on the store for just several thousand dollars of profit a month. Publication of magazines required less hassle and yielded a better financial result. We hardly earned anything on advertising, but earnings from the sales of copies allowed us to thrive and develop. The magazine cost 3 dollars retail – in pre-crisis prices it was 18 rubles, and the wholesale price was 2 dollars (12 rubles). It cost us approximately a dollar to print each copy. We earned $60,000 70,000 gross per month. Taking into account overhead costs and expenses for the editorial staff, we were left with $500,000-600,000 of net profit a year.

At that level, I still didn't have my own car. I wanted a $20,000-30,000 car, but couldn't just go out and buy one. The reason was partly about my priorities: at that time, I allowed myself two types of discretionary spending: to invest in the business and to save some money for retirement. I invested my retirement money in real estate – around 1996, I bought an apartment in Miami, reckoning that its price would rise and, if push came to shove, I could move to the USA. And most of my investments were, so to speak, venture ones: I invested in projects that I thought promising at an early stage, and most of them didn't take off.

Another reason for my frugality was that the trade diverted a large amount of my working capital. Back then, I (like most entrepreneurs) underestimated the importance of cash flow management, and I constantly had cash gaps. I will master the "cash is king" formula later in my career (see details on cash flow management in Chapter 6).

So I rode a bicycle to work, from Kutuzovsky Prospekt to Profsoyuznaya Street. This bicycle, by the way, continued serving me until July 2013, when I got hit by a car. After that accident, the bike was beyond repair.

I could take a small company-owned Ford truck for the weekend. On the one hand, I was proud that I was such a frugal and non-pretentious businessman, but on the other hand, as surprising as it might seem, I never had enough money to buy a good personal car.

I remember how I celebrated my 30th birthday on August 13, 1998. I invited my parents and two company employees to the restaurant. On seeing the bill (I paid 500 dollars for a feast for five people), my father was shocked and said that this money could be used to feed half of Yaroslavl (my hometown). I was pleased to realize that I could afford such luxury. I had the attributes of a successful person of the new epoch: property abroad, Visa and AmEx cards, which hardly anyone saw in Russia back then – and, naturally, my own business.

Chapter 2. Cornered!

In August 1998, my company found itself on the verge of bankruptcy. We were mostly pulled to the bottom by the retail business, which I did not manage to dump in time. We owed our overseas suppliers around a million dollars. However, until August, this debt hadn't worried me much: we purchased goods in bulk and paid for them as we sold off inventory. You might say the company's financial position was ideal: We owned an office (we bought an apartment on the ground floor of the building on Profsoyuznaya Street to use as an office), money in the bank, and accounts receivable that were double our accounts payable. The catch was that our liabilities to our suppliers were in dollars, and our clients owed us rubles.

In several days, the dollar exchange rate rose from 6 rubles to 24 rubles, so my accounts receivable shrank from $2 million to $500,000. Furthermore, my debtors started going bankrupt; not everyone could pay, and $1.7 million simply evaporated. And I still owed a million dollars to my partners overseas.

I had no idea how to pay my suppliers. The demand for the goods, with which our warehouse was packed, fell dramatically. The ruble prices for game consoles, original disks, and cartridges quadrupled. Before the crisis, we were negotiating with the Soyuz retail chain that we would help them start trading video games, but the agreements that we reached were never implemented.

Our media business was also becoming less promising. It became clear that no one would buy a magazine for $3.

Even before the ruble collapsed, I learned from friends that our bank, SBS-Agro, had failed to meet its obligations under a margin call. But it was too late. We could neither take our money out of our bank account nor use it to pay our contractors. We tried to pay the invoices of the printing house, but SBS-Agro was engaged in pure thievery: it provided us with fake documents that allegedly confirmed the transactions, but the money never actually left the bank.

The money that we really had and that I could control was some $20,000 dollars in cash. The situation seemed hopeless: I don't have money to pay my employees, the bank isn't functioning, and there are no earnings. I had absolutely no idea what to do, and I despaired that six years of my painstaking work had gone down the drain.

I remember I felt a burning resentment back then. Firstly, I took offense at the West for deceiving us: The Russian economy was forced into loan addiction, the loans supporting economic development without sufficient internal preconditions. We, the entrepreneurs, were setting our minds on import operations, while local industry was in decline.

Secondly, I took offense at the government, which had allowed the sharp collapse of the ruble, bankrupting many companies and leaving me broke. The government was also to blame for making the banks purchase state treasury bills, and the default dealt a crushing blow to the financial system.

I was extremely angry with our bank too, as it was appropriating our money unscrupulously. Regardless of how the state was treating the banks, it didn't give the banks any right to deceive their clients. I had personal claims against the owner of SBS-Agro, Alexander Smolensky. Now I have begun to understand him a little better, but back then, I felt like a cornered rat: nothing but traitors all around.

It never rains but it pours. In addition to facing problems on all sides in business, my family problems were also exacerbated. My wife and I had had disagreements before, but with the financial crisis, she bluntly declared her wish to end our marriage. When I needed support the most, I was exposed to negative feelings that had been accumulating for years, and heard many compliments – it turned out that I was a wimp, a loser, and a complete schmuck!

I was in despair, broken, and crushed. And it seems to me that despair more or less overwhelmed everyone I knew. I don't remember that any of my acquaintances could brag back then that they knew what to do.

My own naiveté became a separate reason for being upset and blaming myself. After all, I, who considered himself a progressive man, a new-wave entrepreneur, a builder of the new reality, in fact turned out to be an easily bamboozled simpleton. As a businessman, I did not understand the basic principles of how an economy functions. And I had never actually tried to understand them either, boiling it all down to a primitive formula "money – goods – money". It seemed to me that those market laws, which were relevant in the '90s, would never change. Now I started to become more interested in what was happening in the world, and to my great surprise, I realized that paradigm shifts and radical changes in the market happen even in countries with developed economies. This is why the next crisis, which came in 2008 and caught many people napping, was not a surprise to me – I had foreseen it in time and had time to prepare for it.

But let's get back to 1998. As I didn't have any money to pay to my employees, I was about to start firing them, but it turned out that some were ready to work for free, since finding a new job at that difficult time was almost impossible. All of a sudden, I realized that we were living in a different country. Everything that happened to us yesterday no longer mattered in this new reality.

I finally came to terms with the fact that I didn't have any money to repay the debt – I simply acknowledged the fact. To repay a million dollars, I first had to earn it, starting almost from square one. What else could I have started with? My reflections on the new country and the new reality led me to understand one obvious fact: Consumers are now especially sensitive to price, and they are not so devoted to high quality that they can't afford anyway.

We could lower production costs only by cooperating with Russian suppliers, who set their prices in rubles and didn't quadruple them with onset of the crisis. We decided to release a low-budget version of Strana Igr magazine, printing it in a Russian printing house on Russian paper. Back then (even now, I think), there were two types of paper produced in Russia – newsprint paper and offset paper. As far as printing was concerned, we could only use obsolescent printing plants built in the 1980s. To achieve our goal – keeping the magazine's retail price at 18 rubles – we chose newsprint, and printed the cover on offset paper. I invested around $20,000 in this print run – all the money that I had. I risked all I had, and won. But before that, I spent many sleepless nights in the office (nobody was waiting for me at home anyway), when I wasn't sure that I would ever be able to make a living.

Chapter 3. Sacrifice.

My ideas about the shifting consumer preferences turned out to be correct. All the copies were sold out in a couple of hours – despite the plainly cheap delivery and even despite the fact the information in the issue was outdated in places (we started working on it in August). The release of Strana Igr in the new format became a symbol of the fact that we had finally got some action. Naturally, the readers, who had been used to a cool, glossy 240-page magazine, could wrinkle their noses at the sight of a 160-page issue on newsprint. However, in its spirit, it was the same magazine that they had loved. We sent a signal: Life is gradually getting better! And this signal was well accepted. Later, when we had an opportunity, we studied the market of suppliers, found the one who offered offset paper cheaper, and abandoned newsprint.

Having sold the first "crisis" issue, our earnings were not bad, and I thought, why don't we release the next issue not in a month, as usual, but in a week? After all, the editorial staff has been collecting material for "the icebox" since August, and has plenty of it. Because the distributors paid us in cash, we soon released the second issue, and then the third – without establishing any specific periodicity. We didn't manage to re-establish cooperation with the Finnish printing house that printed on glossy paper, because we still owed them for the previous runs, and we were unable to wire foreign currency payments – the banks had not yet returned to regular operations.

By the way, I used all the rubles in my SBS-Agro account to pay taxes many years forward. According to the laws effective at the time, if I instructed the bank to make a payment, I could not be held accountable if the payment failed to arrive. So, the money that was, in fact, frozen in the accounts, and which I could not take out from the bankrupt bank, after all did some good: At least I didn't have to pay taxes on the new earnings – getting them from the bank was now the state's concern.

I started repaying the company's $1 million debt in small portions, starting from several hundred dollars. The suppliers were perplexed, "Dima, you owe us $300,000 and you are paying $100 a month!" I responded, "So it goes; I can't pay more now." We divided all our earnings into three equal portions: The first third went to repay the debt, the second to restore working capital, and I took the last third for my personal needs. I understood that if I "picked the bones" of myself and my employees, there would be no motivation to work. We had to build a new money-making machine, and not give up the shirts off our backs. It was also in the best interests of our lenders, as without this machine we would never have been able to repay our debts.

By November, it became clear that our new printing business had gained momentum, some predictability appeared, and this is when I got nailed. The stress made me ill: Terrible herpes, permanent cold, my skin was peeling off my head in big patches.

A little sports injury, which I got before the events described, became dramatically worse: I had terrible pain in my hand, I even had to call an ambulance, and for another four years, I was addicted to tranquilizers.

The illness completely knocked me off balance for almost a year. I spent 80 % of my time at home, as almost every attempt to get to work caused another attack of the illness. Because my wife had dumped me, one of my employees started taking care of me. Every day he brought me lunch, which he prepared in the office kitchen. My wife never even visited me, and I was very upset by our separation, which I saw as a betrayal on her part.

In August 1999, I got another confirmation that my immune system had been completely compromised. Having gained strength (as it seemed to me), I went to the E3 gaming exhibition in Los Angeles; there I got so sick that I had to admit myself to the hospital. My bills amounted to a thousand dollars a day – back then, it was as distressing for me, as if I had to pay $20,000 a day now. I was so tired of being victimized by my disease, that I decided in despair: That's it, I either have to die or change something in my life! And I chose the second. I had to slowly, painstakingly recover my compromised health, my lost wealth, and my self-respect.

I will remind you that there were still original games and game consoles worth hundreds of thousands of dollars in our warehouse, but the demand for them had declined sharply. Complete hopelessness in the labor market promoted the spirit of entrepreneurship in the company: People who were paid a thousand dollars before, were now motivated to work for one hundred dollars or even for nothing, as it gave them a chance to achieve something by taking on responsibility. This is notably how gamepost.ru, one of the first Russian online stores selling video games, was launched. My employee Alyona Skvortsova, who was entrusted with development of this project, received 100% of the profit during the first year. By the end of the first year, her earnings grew to two or three thousand dollars a month, and I got rid of inventory, got cash to settle my bills with the suppliers, and, at almost zero investment, became the owner of a popular online store. In the second year, Alyona got 50% of the profit, and in the third 30%. It was enough to motivate her to develop the project and build up the earnings.

On seeing how slowly we paid, one of my suppliers agreed to discount the debt: They forgave us 40% of our liabilities on condition that we would pay the remaining amount quickly. To pay them back as fast as possible, I sold my Miami apartment and our office. Truth be told, there was also another reason for selling the office – in the two years since the crisis, our company had grown so much that we needed more room. We rented an office in the center of Moscow, three times larger than the previous one.

By the way, I was not the only one who wanted to repay the debts as quickly as possible. I realized that 80% of my customers (those who were in debt to me before the default), despite a popular opinion that Russian entrepreneurs double-cross each other whenever possible, all paid back as soon as they could. Naturally, they paid in rubles, and the money I got from them wouldn't have been enough to repay what I owed to the suppliers, but my faith in the entrepreneurial community, which had suffered a blow, started to grow stronger. Running ahead of the story, I can say that I signed my last check to a Hong Kong supplier in 2006, meaning that it took us eight years to repay our $1 million debt!

Thinking now about how I reacted to the first serious crisis in my life, I am surprised to realize that I acted almost flawlessly in trying to overcome its consequences. I consider the measures that I took to save my business almost ideal now, when I have many years of experience and the wisdom of life: I quickly abandoned the previous paradigm and adjusted the supply, taking account of shifting market demands; I prevented cash leaks at the critical moment, suspending payment of wages and debt service; I secured restructuring of debt owed to my suppliers, simultaneously making efforts to recover accounts receivable; for some employees, I linked salaries to revenue generated and initiated several entrepreneurial startups inside the company; I formulated clear rules of profit distribution.

The greatest mistake was to sacrifice myself, to economize at my own expense, an inability to protect myself and take care of myself. As a result, stress and fatigue broke my health. It would have been easier to avoid that rather than to rectify the mistake afterwards. Learning from bitter experience, in subsequent crises, I always prioritized my personal interests. I understand that if I don't take care of myself in the first place, I won't have the resources to take care of other people. After all, I am the main source of hope for my business, my employees, and my own family.

The year after the crisis (1999) was for me and many other Russian entrepreneurs a year for a surge of patriotism. The economy, having refocused on import substitution, became less dependent on external factors. We had to work more, we could afford less, but we were happy that we were not living in debt, but on what we earned ourselves. We were overcoming the dependence on the West that had betrayed us.

Chapter 4. Investors.

In this book, I don't follow any chronology, as all the events described in it are important only as examples of critical situations and ways out of them. I spoke about the crisis of 1998 in detail only because it was the first such serious test in my entrepreneurial career, and the most painful of all. In the next decade, my business grew and the culmination of this growth was a merger with our biggest competitor, the Mediasign publishing house. The transaction was closed in August 2008, just weeks before the collapse of Lehman Brothers, which provoked panic in the market and hit the Russian economy. I was expecting this blow, although I could not predict for certain how the world crisis would show itself in our country and affect my business. I had a 20-point action plan and some cash to tide me over in case of more "shit." But I had entertained the possibility of both a fall and growth, so my preparations for a crisis proceeded in parallel to preparation for the M&A deal.

I didn't take a purely defensive position, also because the deal was being financed by investment funds. It meant that I wasn't risking my own money; I just got a minor share in a larger company. That was perfectly fine with me, since I understood that we could optimize operating costs on account of the scale. I was right about that, but wrong about something else. I expected that the investors (who, by the way, didn't share my concerns about the looming crisis and were sure that it would not hit Russia) would become my partners and would support me. Reality turned out to be different: When the company's capitalization fell, the investors decided to shift the blame to me. It became the source of a long, drawn-out conflict, and in the end resulted in our separation. That is how I learned that the mindset of investors has little in common with that of entrepreneurs.

Right after the merger, our company employed 500 people; we were printing 32 magazines, managing 40 websites and one TV channel. Because there now were many specialists on staff with duplicate functions, we could in any case, without any crisis and damage to the business, let a hundred people go and achieve greater efficiency of the merged company. However, in view of the decline of profits and closure of several unprofitable projects, we had laid off around 250 employees by December. Seeing how the deteriorating situation in the economy affected our revenue, I was ready to take even harsher measures to prevent losses. I offered the investors and top managers to transform the company into a very little one, to focus on a few most profitable projects, and even to terminate all activities for a year, freezing the cash for the period of maximum uncertainty. These solutions were not supported, and I started looking for a compromise: I was reducing expenditures a little more and a little earlier than it was really needed.

In the process of the merger, we performed a detailed internal audit of both companies, which greatly facilitated the reduction of expenses in the crisis. We gauged the value of employees for the company, assessed the current status and prospects of each project, performed a complete examination of all expenditures, and held new tenders among suppliers. The first people laid off were those whose influence on the value chain was unclear or could not be measured. Simultaneously, we grasped for any chance to make a profit. Some of our debtors, whose financial solvency was compromised during the crisis, settled their debts through barter – and we happily agreed. Throughout the year, there was a sale in our office of goods received from clients in exchange for the services we provided.

Naturally, I felt awkward towards the investors, because the value of the company that they had just invested in had fallen dramatically in literally just a few months. I suddenly realized that if you have grown for ten years, it doesn't mean that you will necessarily continue growing during the eleventh year too. In fact, even if you have grown for one hundred years in a row, it doesn't give you the right to see a pattern and count on the future growth.

I then placed the investors' interests ahead of my own. Although the fall of the company's capitalization was no fault of mine, I did everything I could to cut the losses. including providing the company with most of my own savings in the form of a loan for replenishment of working capital. Reduction of wages, which affected most employees, affected me and other top managers too – we started getting 30% less.

Talking to investors after the crisis had set in, I noticed a striking and unexpected change in their behavior. I came to the conclusion that entrepreneurs often misunderstand investors and their roles, which leads to conflict.

First of all, we should understand that professional investors manage other people's money, and not just money but capital. The investor's priority is not to lose money (naturally, I am not referring to venture investments, but to private equity). Fear of losing money doesn't go along with the entrepreneurial spirit, where risks and failures are ordinary things on one's way to success.

Employees of investment companies who work for a salary are less prone to entrepreneurial thinking. I believe they aren't even investors, since they don't invest their own money. Hired specialists don't necessarily care about the interests of their clients (the owners of capital). Mostly, as with any other hired employees, they are interested in not tarnishing their career with some unfortunate decision. Therefore, one shouldn't expect daring steps from such employees – for them, it is better to do nothing than to make a mistake. When a crisis comes, most employees of investment funds have a panic attack. They understand that in the immediate years ahead, they can't expect to make especially profitable investments, and the management will, in all likelihood, blame them for the fact that the value of the assets they invested in has fallen. Any real investor understands that loss of some of a company's value is normal in a market economy. But, nonetheless, everyone wants to report only successes.

The conflict between entrepreneurs and investors is mostly based not on personal complaints, but on false expectations. The entrepreneur whose company is experiencing a crisis is under stress and needs support. He naively supposes that the investor who has invested in his company is a partner, who has agreed to share not only the profits, but the risks as well. For investors, it would really be logical to support the entrepreneur, as that is the person who is the mainstay of the company, and the security of investments depends on whether the entrepreneur will be able to handle the challenges of a crisis period. But in practice, it often happens the other way around: investors (or employees of an investment fund) impose their anxiety and vexation on entrepreneurs, don't relieve their problems, but make their lives harder. I advise entrepreneurs who take the investments to keep in mind that in 90% of cases, the investors' reaction to an external or internal crisis will take the form of reprimands, complaints, and pressure.

I needed a month to understand that several of my investors were more focused on risks than on creative development. When I realized this clearly, I decided that we had different agendas, and it was time to bid farewell. I only had to agree on the terms of how I would buy back my share in the company. Here the crisis has its upsides: When the company is cheaper, it's easier for you to regain control over it. If you don't have the money at that moment to buy your company out, try to sell your share. Anyway, maintaining relations with the investors who have grown disappointed in the project and are projecting their disappointment on you, is the less constructive way out of crisis. Internal conflicts and disagreements can ruin a company, so it's better to get the money while you still can.

Coming back to the question of disappointed expectations, I would like to note that the investor's job is to give money. You shouldn't expect the investor to be actively involved in the management of the company. Especially if you're dealing with hired employees of investment funds – most of them are people with financial education, who have little understanding about how business works. If investors are not qualified to do so, they should not be allowed to participate in the company's management, and there are special tools to make sure of that, such as limitation of the right to vote at the meeting of the board of directors and to intervene in operational management. If you are lucky to find an investor who knows his way around in business, it a great advantage, but I still recommend looking at that as a pleasant addition to the investors' main function, and not one of their duties. I have heard entrepreneurs complain that the investor who has invested in the company "doesn't do any work." It should be understood that professional investors, who are able to not only invest money, but to ensure its security and growth with their subsequent smart moves, are but a few percent of the total. As a rule, they are former and current entrepreneurs.

I have been lucky to cooperate with investors from various countries, including a Scandinavian company that manages family capital, a Russian company that invests the money of American owners, as well as a Japanese company with Japanese money.

When I was ready to bring an investor in for the first time, I specially instructed my investment banker not to consider Anglo-Saxon companies. It seemed to me that they are ideologically distant from my business, and are not oriented toward cooperation. In the end, we managed to attract exactly the type of investor I had been dreaming of – a Scandinavian company, whose values were close to the values of my business. It was easy for us to find a common language, but the Scandinavian partners turned out to be risk-averse, and at the first signs of problems, they decided to sell their share.

With my second investor (an "Anglo-Saxon" one according to my classification system, since their money was American and the principles for managing it too), the dialog was purely about numbers. Business efficiency was the only criterion that shaped their attitude toward me. If business prospers, I'm a great guy; but if we faced some difficulties and the numbers declined, then I was a sucker. Such investors mostly protect their own interests and are ready to disregard the entrepreneur's interests. If they have a legitimate opportunity to take away your business or property, they will do so, without a doubt. Nothing personal – they are just saving their money.

Japanese investors turned out to be the most amazing partners. They are very careful, so the decision-making process can take them several years. But when the decision is made, the value of the partnership is no longer discussed. If the partner behaves decently, even bad business results are not a reason for criticism and termination of relations. A Japanese investor is ready to face all the challenges together with the entrepreneur. One can only dream about such an investor!

SUMMARY

How to avoid problems with investors at a time of crisis.

1. Hire good investment lawyers; don't spare money on them.

2. Set aside cash in advance for repurchase of your share.

3. Be ready for conflict with investors; don't see them as your partners, whose goals and objectives match yours.

Chapter 5. A paradigm shift.

In 1991, when I started going to China, there was a total deficit of everything on the Russian market. In addition to unsatisfied demand for basic goods, the country didn't have many things that had become ordinary in the global market. This period provided a unique opportunity to entrepreneurs: You could both saturate the market with basic goods and form new niches, introduce consumers for the first time to world-class products. Remember the phenomenal hours-long lines at the first McDonald's that opened in Moscow in 1990. What was so special about the American fast-food offer? It wasn't meat and bread – the main ingredients of the Big Mac – that caused such a frenzy in Muscovites. But associating oneself with the Western lifestyle really meant a lot.

In this market paradigm, I built a retail business by importing new goods that had not yet become mundane – video games. But in several years, games turned into mass entertainment and the paradigm changed. Now people wanted cheap games, and I had to decide what to do next – flood the market with cheap game consoles or focus on elite gamers who prefer buying the original products. In neither case did I have an opportunity already to surprise anybody with the novelty and uniqueness of my offer. There was a third way: To make a media product for a big community of people playing bootleg games. The last option was the most profitable one, and I left the retail business without regret.

The crisis of 1998 brought another paradigm shift in the consumer market. People's earnings fell dramatically, and a low price became the main requirement for a mass-market product. In the next several years, demand changed under the influence of several factors at once: Gradual growth of wealth, rapid development of the Internet, and spread of digital technologies. By that time, we had acquired expertise in niche media and reacted to the trend by launching several projects aimed at all kinds of enthusiasts – not only gamers and hackers, but gadget lovers, car owners, etc.

In the next decade, the approach to media consumption changed. Hyperactivity of advertisers meant that thick, glossy magazines, which are very expensive to produce, became free or very cheap. With numerous online mass media appearing, people became convinced that information should be free. This paradigm started collapsing after the 2008 crisis, when incomes also fell, and advertisers became much more economical and selective. This forced many mass media outlets to leave the market; only the top periodicals remained that managed to retain their advertisers, as well as niche products that never suffered from the lack of advertising, or could readjust quickly and find a new business model. Our publishing house's projects always gravitated towards narrow niches, so the share of survivors among us was higher, yet the blow was significant. We couldn't ignore the advertising paradigm, and for some time, we accepted the rules played by the whole market. When the rules changed, some of our projects became unprofitable and were closed down; the remaining ones had to fight for survival. This is how we ended up in the current paradigm: We produce the content that consumers will pay for.

My example is a case history of how an entrepreneur is forced to react to the shifting market paradigm. We had to change both the industry and the business model within that same industry. External crises (like those of 1998 and 2008) can accelerate the shifting of paradigms, because they affect consumers' behavior and macroeconomic conditions. However, the paradigm can change at any moment and without global shocks. Unpredictability and sometimes even a lack of logic are characteristic features of this phenomenon. Could anybody in 2010 have foreseen the quick collapse of RIM, the producer of Blackberry, which was the de facto standard of mobile communication for corporate users? The company's shares grew, as did sales. It seemed that RIM had everything necessary to retain leadership in its segment: patents, high-quality products, focus on confidentiality of information, and an army of loyal users. However, all those advantages became insignificant in view of the capabilities of iPhone, which, at first sight, was created more for entertainment than for serious work.

And what research could indicate that Russians would love sushi? Let's consider it for a moment: Japanese culture is not popular in our society; we don't eat much rice, don't like raw fish, and don't cook with ginger. And then, all of a sudden, out of the whole Japanese cuisine, everybody started to love sushi! The progressing Russian nationalism and an inclination to see Muslims as a threat are perfectly compatible with the love of the hookah that appeared out of thin air. Now an Italian restaurant has to have both a sushi bar and a hookah. Let's agree, it is a complete nut-house! But this is the market paradigm for today's Russian restaurateurs.

New paradigms take shape under the influence of an unpredictable combination of many factors. When the old paradigm stops working, you rarely have a clear understanding of what new opportunities have the biggest potential. For instance, when my retail business lost its profitability, the choice in favor of media was one of many possible, and not necessarily the best. I could have rebuilt the retail business, focused on another consumer group, sold other products, or master new trades. And it is quite possible that having made another choice, I could have reached at least the same level of success or even higher. Realizing that, I can't give anyone a precise recommendation regarding selection of a new paradigm. To make the best choice, you need to take a broad look at the world, read a lot, talk to people, and, ideally, engage in many types of activities. If you understand that the old paradigm has run dry, ask yourself the question, "Where is my focus?" Every choice brings possibilities and risks. Switching to something new, you can lose your grounding in the area where you are the most experienced, and not achieve the same success in the new paradigm. In any case, if you decide to shift the paradigm, don't count on high earnings right away from your new business. This is exactly why new projects are better launched while the old ones are still profitable and allow you to pay for your experiments.

All experiments are valuable, because you learn something from them. However, their effect may turn out to be different than what you expected. For instance, one of the new paradigms is social networks, the craze for which spread like an epidemic. Thousands of entrepreneurs from all over the world attempted to get rich by launching their social networks. Most of them have not become and are unlikely to ever become profitable.

But people who believed in this paradigm and started working in it, acquired competencies that can be used elsewhere, such as for earning money on Facebook.

SUMMARY

How to react to a paradigm shift.

1. Analytical methods don't allow one to forecast a paradigm shift in the market.

2. The choice of a new industry or business model is never obvious.

3. Rapid movements, such as changing the industry, are risky. Think how you can effectively use the experience you have acquired, in the new paradigm.

4. When changing the paradigm of your business, don't expect quick profit.

Chapter 6. Cash flow.

When I was only starting out in business, my knowledge in finance was just enough to calculate the difference between the purchase price and the retail price. I came to China, saw a game console, and thought, "Wow! I will buy it here for $30, sell it in Russia for $100, and earn $70. I am rich!"

It never occurred to me that transport expenses raise the price of the product significantly. I also didn't take into account the fact that Chinese game consoles are not very reliable; some of them will inevitably break. At that stage, despite the seemingly huge margin, I never had enough money. I borrowed working capital from my friends and relatives at huge interest rates. I remember that I got my first loan at 20% a week. At the beginning of 1990s, these were acceptable terms and I could recover these interest payments. But when the market started becoming saturated and the margin fell, my income fell sharply. Lack of working capital meant that the goods people wanted were not to be found on the shelves of my stores. This led me to the necessity of automating warehouse inventory management, which was done, but I still didn't understand the idea of cash flow or balance. I could find my way around a balance sheet to some extent – I loved to verify how much cash I had, how many goods I had in stock, and I estimated the net asset value. But I couldn't grasp the concept of cash flow. I didn't consider that time was passing, rental payments were piling up, cargo was in transit – and all of that takes money. To sell goods worth $100,000 a month, you need $200,000 in cash. And if I earn $20,000 in profit, I have to leave all the profit in the business and not take it out until I accumulate sufficient working capital. Instead, I invested all the profit in new stores and dubious business projects, which often didn't fit in with my retail business development strategy.

This was one of the reasons my stores were less profitable than they could have been, as I now realize. I remember my Hong Kong supplier admonishing me, "Don't expand so fast, you need cash." I didn't listen to him, kept on doing it my own way, and once a critical moment came: I couldn't pay wages and rent. Deciding that the business had become unprofitable and hopeless, I closed three stores out of five, and took the remaining stock to the two stores that were left. At once, the picture changed radically: all the necessary goods were always available, the profitability of the two outlets rose sharply. I realized for the first time that it's not enough to have a product that is in demand and can bring profit. It should be available on the shelf, and not only available, but in abundance. You need cash for that.

In 1999, when the company had already become a publisher and was recovering from the crisis, I came back to the topic of cash flow and invited in a consultant from London. He helped us develop a financial strategy and set up spreadsheets for financial indicators, including cash flow. My CFO started carefully making sure that the company had a financial cushion – he authorized reluctantly (or not at all) payments that didn't relate to transactions that brought immediate profit. By 2003, this cushion had reached $1 million, but it didn't prevent us from attracting investments in the amount of $2 million, most of which was aimed at replenishment of working capital. At some point, I started to realize that sitting on a cash pile just to prevent a cash gap makes no sense. To have a surplus of cash is a dream of every financial director, as he will never have any problems. But from the point of view of the business owner or the investor, it is an inefficient use of money. Naturally, our money surplus didn't lie dormant – we put it in deposit accounts and got some risk-free income. Such an ultra-conservative strategy can be justified in some cases, but for an ambitious company in a growing market, it hinders development.

Under the influence of Australian financial guru Alan Miltz, I developed a more deliberate approach to cash flow management. I first heard him at an entrepreneurial conference in Marrakesh in 2006; a year later, we met again in Tokyo. Not on the first try, but I started to understand the importance of cash flow – I should say that not only most entrepreneurs, but also most professional finance managers, don't know how to calculate cash flow. According to Alan, 90% of entrepreneurs throughout the world are focused on profit and loss accounts, which don't give a full picture of the enterprise's finances. Very often in business, finished products are delivered for sale based on deferred payment terms, but if a batch of products is ordered from a factory, full or partial advance payment is required. To finance this gap, the enterprise needs an amount of cash equal to several months of revenue. To get the money, we ask the bank for a loan, pay high interest rates, and, depending on the size of margin, we can get zero or negative profit. If the entrepreneur can't calculate the cash flow, he won't even understand what led him to bankruptcy, whether the business was really unprofitable or a formally profitable company that fell victim to a cash gap.

I made the decision to launch new projects using only investors' money, but neither my personal funds nor loans. This approach allowed me to ensure a balance of interests: we always had enough cash and we didn't have to hold back the company's development. However, my interest in the topic of cash flow management didn't cease, and I continued to study (mostly with Alan, whom I even invited to Moscow to conduct a financial audit of my company) and to gain experience. I am sure that it was precisely the focus on cash flow management that enabled our company to withstand the hard times after the 2008 crisis, when earnings fell sharply and the market started to demonstrate painful processes relating to the paradigm shift (see previous chapter).

One of the discoveries that I made in the process of studying the company's finances was that most CFOs don't want and can't profoundly understand the business that they are trying to manage. They can't talk to a business owner in a common language, aren't able to explain in a simple way the meaning of the reports that they prepare, and don't know how to use these reports to increase business efficiency. I know exactly what I am talking about, as I have interviewed approximately 70 candidates for the position of CFO. Only one of them fitted our needs and worked for several years with us. During these years, I came to the conclusion that companies with turnover less than $100 million don't require a CFO. It's better to hire an expensive consultant (like the same Alan Miltz or another consultant of mine, Andre Gien from the USA), who will create a management accounting system customized for your business. Then you have to program it in the accounting software used in your company (we use 1C), and every month bring in two auditors to analyze the indicators (you won't have to spend more than $1,000-2,000 on that). If the primary data is entered carefully and punctually, you will always have fresh, absolutely trustworthy data on cash flow movement, profits and losses, etc. You will be able to identify beforehand that, for instance, next month you can expect a cash gap, so you either need to withhold outgoing payments, or take a loan, or collect accumulated debts in a hurry. This is exactly the kind of system that I am using right now, and I believe that the quality of my financial management is now higher than at any time in the past. Several tens of thousands of dollars spent on hiring world-class consultants and 1C programming paid off rather quickly, as the salary of a good CFO is $10,000 per month and higher. If you are lucky enough to find a really good CFO, he/she will do the same thing (set up an automated accounting system), and then will have to invent tasks for themselves in order not to sit around doing nothing. There are not likely to be any new indicators in your business each month that must be reflected in the reporting. Naturally, to manage without a CFO, you will need basic knowledge of finance, and I urge you to not begrudge the time and money spent on your education – it is an important investment in yourself and in your business.

I would like to note that my seeking foreign consultants' advice was caused by a necessity: I simply hadn't met any professionals of that caliber in Russia. I had turned to famous consulting companies that operate in the local market, but found them to have the same shortcomings that I saw in most CFOs: they don't understand their clients' business. By working with such a company, you will find a consultant with a financial education, who has never built a business and who generates financial reports formally, without accounting for the unique features of a specific business. For instance, if a company has a service subdivision that provides services to other departments, the consultant with a formal approach may post the expenses for maintenance of this business unit to different cost items, but will never ask himself some questions: Are all the functions of this unit really necessary? Would it not be better to outsource these functions? Would it make sense to turn this unit into an individual business unit that would invoice internal clients? As a result, the expense structure that you will get won't contain the information that will help you optimize these costs. Extra costs turn out to be implicit, disguised, spread out in a thin layer through all departments of the company. High-quality financial reports can only be prepared by a specialist with direct business management experience as well as profound knowledge of finance. The above-mentioned Andre Gien, founder of Global Finance Bridge, spent a month at our company preparing reports; he met and talked to the head of every business unit. Until he fully grasped all the business processes, he did not even start to prepare the reports.

SUMMARY

The principles of financial management

1. Cash flow is the most important indicator of the company's financial health, which is mostly ignored by entrepreneurs.

2. Identify the volume of working capital you need (as a rule, it equals several months worth of revenue) and leave all the profit in the business until you have that necessary amount at your disposal.

3. The CFO who wants and can understand the essence of your business is a rare find. Invest in your own financial education.

4. Automate financial accounting and planning by attracting world-class consultants. In the end, you will get financial reports of better quality at less cost.

Chapter 7. Top managers.

I remember how I called in my top managers for an anti-crisis committee back in 2008. One of the items on the agenda was the future of unprofitable projects. "Let's shut them all down," I suggested. To which the top manager responsible for operational management replied, "I didn't come to this company to shut down projects. I need scale." The actual wording might have been different, but this was the gist of his answer. The number of employees was more important to him than the amount of profit. Let the company lose money, but he will stay in charge of a large organization for another year or so.

We soon parted ways, but I continued watching the development of his career. At his next job, everything was repeated – hiring an enormous number of new employees, rapid expansion against despite rising losses, and pulling the wool over the investors' eyes.

There is a popular employee classification that was not invented by me, which says that you employ "predators", "parasites", "owners"," and "sheep". Among top managers, the only ones you won't meet are from the last category: "sheep" have neither ambitions nor talents to rise up the career ladder; they are empty-headed clerks who take no initiative.

A crisis is the time when the best and the worst qualities manifest themselves most clearly in employees. This applies to top managers too. To react properly to their behavior, you first have to know whom you are dealing with.

The "predator's" real goal is to get his piece of the pie. He is willing to put his company on the line for his personal benefit. It doesn't matter to him what losses you, his employer, incur, as long as he is "in clover." He takes kickbacks, he takes money from your pocket (for instance, paying for his personal purchases with a corporate card), and abuses the authority that has been delegated to him. He can take the post offered to him simply for a line in his resume, not showing any loyalty or genuine interest in your business. A person like that clearly separates his own interests from those of the company's.

The "parasite" tries to work less – he either can't or doesn't want to or both. All his energy is spent on maintaining the status quo: He huffs and puffs to show you how hard he works. But his real contribution is not worth the remuneration that he gets for his work.

"Owners" are the smallest group of top managers. They do everything they can for your business to succeed, treating it as if it were their own.

In "peacetime", parasites and predators try not to show their true identity by pretending to be caring "owners". The business owner who hired them may even have no idea what kind of people are on his management team. A crisis inevitably places more stress on top managers, and the business owner can expect some unpleasant discoveries. If you have suddenly identified a "predator" or a "parasite", they should be fired immediately, even though they may seem to be experienced professionals and pivotal figures in many processes. Of course, if a person has reached the status of a top manager, that person must be "terrific" at something. But a crisis situation is different because manifestations of predatoriness or parasitism will only get worse. You can't find a less auspicious moment to start cultivating an attitude "ownership" in your people.

In a crisis, top managers are best described by their actions. People who take care of the company's interests don't separate themselves from it. For instance, if top managers fire people but are unable to part with their own secretaries and assistants, sacrificing their own interests, it should get your attention. The top manager who can help your company overcome the crisis can be identified by specific actions: Efficient cost reduction, successful search for reserves to increase revenue. You should immediately part company with those who can't do such things. The good thing about a crisis is that it provides you with an opportunity to check people's loyalty in combat conditions, when one doesn't have to show one's eloquence and build beautiful graphs of future earnings, but must save the company with a day-to-day work. I urge business owners not to keep people on their team based on their past achievements and on the premise that you might need their skills in the future, when the situation normalizes. Hiring a top manager is a difficult and expensive task; therefore, there may be a great temptation to have "your own" person on the team. But the managers who demonstrate insufficient loyalty and zeal in a crisis are also disloyal and lacking in zeal in "peacetime"; you simply might not have noticed it. Furthermore, if you find yourself in a crisis, you will have to transform the company in order to survive until peacetime comes. Disloyal employees will most likely hold you back and be a hindrance in this process. Besides, the configuration of a company in the process of getting out of a crisis can change so much that there will be no place left in it for your current top managers. I believe that it's better to fire a person right away whose value you doubt, and then hire him again when he is needed (or another specialist of the same type) – even for a higher salary, if you have to entice him to return. It is important to remember that most hired employees are bought for money; very few work with you out of extreme loyalty. You should also understand that people will try to manipulate you, to make you pity them, but the only criterion for evaluating their importance for the team must be productivity.

In a crisis, the role of the company owner usually increases. You could hope that the hired top manager will behave like an owner and will handle the situation. If that happens, support that top manager and take good care of him. But as far as I can judge, in most cases it doesn't happen. My observations show that when the hard times come, in practice, the company owner becomes more active in business management – just because he is the boss and he can't look on indifferently as his business falls apart before his very eyes. You can't expect that the top manager, even one who sincerely wishes to help the company, will strain every sinew to preserve the property of another person. Personalities like Lee Iacocca are very rare. Naturally, we would like to have more of them, and we can contribute somewhat to an owner-like attitude by encouraging our people and promising them significant gains if the crisis is resolved. They can be remunerated by a share in the profits or a share of the business. And here, by the way, you have another opportunity to identify a "parasite" or a "predator". If a top manager does not agree to accept future profits or a share in the company as compensation for a temporary reduction in salary (let's say the company already has serious financial difficulties and you are forced to cut wages and salaries, while demanding even more dedication), it means this person is not an "owner". By rejecting a proposal like that, the person lets you know that he doesn't believe that the business can become profitable and grow in value; he confirms his inability to affect the financial result, and also tells you that he is not prepared to share your burdens. Decide for yourself whether you want such a manager on your team.

Remember that your commitments to your employees are only worth something if they are counterbalanced by the employees' commitments to you. In the previous paragraph, I wrote that the owner of the company shouldn't expect hired top managers to have the same attitude as the owner and give it all they've got. However, I believe that a strictly formal attitude on the part of a top manager is unacceptable, especially in a crisis. If I hear my top manager, responding to my request to deal with a problem urgently, say, "Sorry, I get off work at five," I conclude immediately that the person is not up to the job. A top manager is called a "top manager" because he will go above and beyond the call of duty at a tough moment. The lack of desire to go beyond one's formal job description shows that the person is lacking in the instinct for self-preservation. It's best to get rid of such people.

When I say the owner should take an active role, I don't necessarily mean that the owner starts fulfilling functions previously delegated to his top managers. An active role can take many forms. For instance, the company owner can identify functions and business processes that have become redundant. In one of the critical situations, when there was a dramatic decline of revenue, I decided to radically simplify the company's organizational structure, get rid of several legal entities, and by doing so, reduce the service personnel and administrative costs. After restructuring, the company's finances became so simple that I myself or my assistant could easily manage them. Our CFO (who is unquestionably a much better financial expert than me), agreed with the obvious: There was nothing left to do in the company that required his professional competence. Could he have initiated such restructuring of the company on his own? I doubt it, because he would have eliminated his own job. Did I have to carry the burden of the CFO's functions? Not really, because the functions became totally different. Even if I single-handedly handled management accounting and similar tasks, the labor intensity of these processes can't be compared to the load carried by the CFO when the company was larger and more complex.

As a rule, anti-crisis decisions must be made and implemented quickly; for this reason, you could benefit greatly from an anti-crisis committee with invited anti-crisis managers. The costs of setting up such a committee and attracting outside managers with the competencies that you require at that time usually pay for themselves, as this structure doesn't exist for a long time, but is called upon to solve the most pressing problems: cost optimization, search for new growth drivers, etc. It is very useful to have people on your team who can take a fresh look at the situation from the outside – not only because you and your managers have gotten used to do everything in a certain way, but also because it is impossible to know everything. If you have an opportunity, don't hesitate to ask help from an entrepreneur who has built a larger business and has already faced the problems that you are experiencing right now. Such people can also often give you personal advice (I was given such advice, even for free) and recommend specialists that you should hire to deal with specific challenges.

At the end of this chapter, I will say a few words about people who are co-owners of the business to some extent. They are either top managers who received shares in the company as an incentive, but didn't pay for their share themselves, or they are investors who invested their own money. The latter can be both passive co-owners (not participating in operational management) and active co-owners (for instance, members of the board of directors and top managers).

My rule is not to shift problems onto my partners, but to rely only on myself. Naturally, if you have a partner in the business, you have a moral right to come to ask him for help in the hard times, but you shouldn't expect your partner to be a strong crisis manager or a backup funding source. Earlier, by bringing a partner into my business, I thought I was making my business stronger, because I would have an additional resource in any unpredictable situation. However, my experience showed that it's not necessarily so. Although one should logically expect that partners would be vitally interested in saving the business, in practice, people's roles in a crisis don't really change. The manager who received a small block of shares as a reward for his performance, in most cases retains the mentality of a hired manager, so in a crisis, it is unlikely that he will surpass other managers in his ingenuity and self-sacrifice. It's more likely that he will be nervous and regret that the company's capitalization has declined, than fight for it as if it were his own property.

SUMMARY

How should one build relations with hired top managers in a crisis?

1. Take the opportunity to identify "parasites" and "predators".

2. Judge top managers by their actions: decisions, productivity, and financial results.

3. Don't keep a top manager on your team whom you can do without right now, even if you value him highly.

4. Motivate top managers by offering them a generous share of the profits or a share in the company after the negative trend has been overcome.

5. The owner's role in a crisis increases.

6. Attract managers from outside the company to your anti-crisis committee.

Chapter 8. Employees.

These events took place in September 2012. I had a regular planned meeting with the editor-in-chief of one of the automotive magazines printed by Gameland. And, as is my habit, I didn't forget to probe his situation: "How is your work going? What are your plans for the coming year? Are there any problems?" The editor told me he wanted to develop the website and another new, but very promising, publishing project. "Everything is cool!" he told me. He had already been working at the company for five years.

Our next meeting took place in October. I couldn't believe my ears, when I heard him say, "I am leaving in two weeks. I believe it will be better for the magazine, because we have started to stagnate. I promise to hand over my responsibilities properly. My subordinate Vasya will do just fine. By the way, I didn't have a chance to use my paid leave this year, so I will do it right now." And the next day, he went on vacation, without handing over his responsibilities.

We handled this situation with great difficulty and ensured the uninterrupted release of the magazine after the sudden resignation of a key employee. But I still wanted to understand what had happened. Ok, he resigned, it was his right. But why, just one month before that, was he assuring me that he loved the job and was full of creative plans? So I invited him for a cup of coffee.

"Look, I performed my duties, but you didn't," he told me. "My paychecks were delayed."

To tell you the truth, this new version also didn't impress me much. We had had regular delays in salaries and wages, sometimes long, sometimes short, since 2009. So the real reasons were probably different. His sudden resignation makes me think that his real goal was to inflict damage. Probably, he had accumulated some resentments. The fact that after leaving Gameland he changed his profession, may mean that he didn't enjoy the job of an editor-in-chief.

Being a hired employee is a life choice and a psychology. Hired employees can work with pleasure at your company, their efforts can make you rich, but it doesn't make them your partners. Why? Evidently because they don't take responsibility for the company's survival and its earnings. They don't really care much whether you make profits or losses – what matters is being paid on time.

My big mistake was that I gladly shared profits with my employees during periods of prosperity and tried to share losses with them in times of crisis. However, I don't consider partnership relations with employees a mistake. Sooner or later, the hired employee can mature enough to become an entrepreneur (I have already given examples in this book and will continue to do so). My mistake was that I decided to use this approach when I saw fit, without discussing it with my employees. Naturally, nobody objected to getting a share of profits, whereas losses unfailingly turned out to be my personal problem.

The problem was, of course, that my expectations were inappropriate. The employees conducted themselves perfectly appropriately, in full accord with their nature. There is nothing offensive about their attitude.

In the previous chapter, I spoke about the behavior of top managers in a crisis. What about rank-and-file employees? I distinguish among several typical scenarios.

There is a category of highly professional employees who can easily find a job – especially when our company is going through a local crisis, but the balance of supply and demand in the labor market is not changing much. Usually such people resign if any parameter of their employment deteriorates (reduction of salary, contraction of benefit package contraction, increased demands, etc.).

In fact, these people are service providers and they should expect a corresponding attitude towards themselves. Don't count on their willingness to tighten their belts. If you value what they do, carefully respect all original agreements – or, if that is impossible, discuss the changed conditions.

Employees from the second category can benefit from the crisis. They know that there will be layoffs, there will be many unhappy people, but they understand that the company will still have resources that could be beneficial to them. For example, they may view other people's departure as a unique chance for their own career growth, and scheme to achieve their goals. They are ready to criticize their colleagues and come up with some proposals to distinguish themselves in your eyes. They will say how much they support you, hoping that their salary will remain intact during a general cutback, or, at least, that they will not be fired. Building relations with such employees can be a rather challenging task, mostly because you don't understand their real motivation. And when you hear them make some unexpected proposal, you can't figure out how you should react to it. But people of this category can be identified by the fact that their behavior has changed.

The most unpleasant type of employees in a crisis are the whiners. They are people who usually don't do much good for the company, who, for some personal reasons feel humiliated or inferior; they are miserable and spiteful. They suppressed all these negative emotions when the situation was normal, but when the company that employs them starts having problems, these people can't control their tempers anymore and pour out all their pain on those around them. The reason for their complaints and outrage is not the crisis – the crisis merely opens the door for an internal emotional storm.

I tentatively call such employees "polizei", like the polizei recruited by the Nazis from among Soviet citizens during World War II, who immediately started persecuting their own countrymen, having been quite inconspicuous before the war and never having opposed the system. Only when the Germans arrived did their accumulated malice find an outlet. Something similar takes place in the company that is going through a crisis. The "offended ones", who had previously kept a low profile, start spreading gossip and gloomy speculation.

There are many managers who think that dissatisfied team members are beneficial, because they help reveal shortcomings and improve the enterprise's performance. They say that if there are no dissatisfied people, then you have surrounded yourself with sycophants who always play along. But there is an essential difference. There are people who criticize to make the company better. Their criticism is constructive, and usually they have something to propose. However, if the critic only complains and doesn't suggest anything, it sends a signal to me: This person should be fired promptly in order to separate the healthy part of the team from his demoralizing influence. In a crisis, you need to reform your company. To do that, you need to be able to rely on people, and the harm from the alarmist is not compensated by any possible benefit that he could provide at his workplace. Even if other employees don't listen to him, the eternal complainer simply poisons the atmosphere, makes things uncomfortable for everyone, and taints the image of your company.

And, finally, there are employees who don't complain. The job that was good enough for them in the past, and is still good enough in a crisis. They perceive difficulties with understanding and don't see any reason to leave the company or to feel discouraged. Congratulations on having such employees; they also deserve congratulations for successfully passing the crisis test. With this team, you will build your business anew.

It is also possible that in a crisis your people will need to acquire new skills. For example, you are in the process of a paradigm shift (see Chapter 5) or you have reduced the number of employees in service units, but you have vacancies in other departments. Employees can react differently to the proposal that they master something new, unusual for them. Some people agree and master it, others refuse, don't show any enthusiasm, and demonstrate their ineptitude. These will probably be lost to you: Unwillingness or inability to adapt will lead to them becoming alien elements in the company – they will either understand that on their own or you will have to show them. However, there is no reason to hurry up and lay them off. If there is still work for a loyal employee who is not ready to embrace the changes, let him work. I try to not lay off such people at the peak of a crisis; I tell them that they can work with assurance for another year, for example, as long as there is a need for the business processes within the old, obsolete paradigm. The person knows what awaits him, he can take his time searching for a new job, and there is a chance of preserving good relations.

Those who are willing to change along with the company should be treated as the most valuable asset, and you shouldn't forget to reward them when the financial situation allows it.

A crisis is a time of bad news, and business owners and top managers are constantly faced with the question: What information should be shared with employees? Should there be a policy of maximum openness, or is it better to protect morale and not spread panic? I follow this rule: If I know about a serious deterioration in the situation now or in the future, and the employees don't know about it yet, I don't tell them about what they can't change. The reason for that decision lies in what I have written about above: Hired employees are not your partners; they didn't want to take risks and we didn't agree to share responsibility. Making them aware of the deteriorating business situation will not make it any better. The only thing they really want to know is what is going to happen to them: Whether they will be fired, whether their wage or salary may be delayed, whether they may be moving to a new office.

But if negative information has already reached the employees and has caused rumblings of discontent in the team, I describe the situation as is, with full understanding that it might not sound comforting. As for possible consequences – layoffs, wage and salary reduction or delay – I also present the worst-case scenario: "It's the worst thing that could happen to us." And this is good enough to help relieve the tension: employees know what they should be afraid of and what they shouldn't.

Key employees deserve your trust – they should get more information from you. Your subsequent actions won't catch them by surprise, and, besides, they can participate in making anti-crisis decisions. However, you shouldn't count too much on the latter. If people wanted to make decisions, they would have done it in "peacetime" too. But if that didn't happen, this capability would hardly emerge in a crisis.

I started this chapter with a description of one of the regular meetings with my employee. I hold such "diagnostic" meetings at least once a month in order to be aware of how they are doing and be able to support them individually. Experience has proven that everybody has quite different reasons for worries and discontent. In the above-described case, my diagnostics failed, but in other cases, similar meetings helped identify a problem in the making and allowed me to take action to alleviate tension.

SUMMARY

How to practice team-building in a crisis.

1. If you want to avoid disappointment, don't regard hired employees as responsible partners who treasure your business.

2. Categorize your employees by their reactions to a crisis – "suppliers" who are sensitive to worsening conditions, opportunists, whiners, and loyal team members who may or may not be prepared to change their responsibilities, if necessary.

3. Encourage constructive criticism, but get rid of those who only complain without proposing anything.

4 Don't hesitate to withhold information about a deteriorating business situation from the whole team, if team members can't affect it anyway. If everyone knows about the problems, present the worst-case scenario to contain negative emotions.

5. Share more information with key employees and don't forget to ask about their well-being.

Chapter 9. Internal entrepreneurship.

As a fan of entrepreneurship, I have long thought that other people also dream and should create their own businesses. And, enjoying a certain level of respect from my employees, I tried to cajole some of them into entrepreneurship. Later I learned that fewer than 1% of people in the world are able to become entrepreneurs, and I came to terms with the fact that most people are not willing to take risks. But before that, with my blessing, employees of mine undertook various entrepreneurial initiatives in the company; that happened right during crises, when resources were no longer needed and I was faced with a choice: to part ways with people or help them start their own businesses. I can't claim that these initiatives had a strictly positive influence on my business, but I find the experience to have been very useful.

The first example of "forced" entrepreneurship in Gameland was mentioned in Chapter 3 – in 1999, my employee launched an online video games store. In 2009, knowing of the difficult situation in the labor market, I proposed to the employees, who were being made redundant, to use the vacated workplaces and infrastructure (accounting, legal aid, consulting) to start their own businesses. My call was answered by around twenty people, and some of them are still in the business they launched back then: an event agency and a couple of online stores.

When I allowed my employees to use the company's resources for their own projects, it wasn't purely altruism from my side. I hoped that these projects would develop, become profitable, and my share in them (which I got in return for providing the resources) in time would turn into a source of passive income. These expectations were not borne out. At the second stage, when some of these companies started generating revenue, I started getting small amounts from them for workplace rent, which I had provided for free earlier. Only one project generated profit, but it was modest – around $1,000 per month.

Looking back, I don't regret that I supported my former employees' entrepreneurial initiatives, but I must admit that all this was more my way of caring for them, than a profit-making machine built on the model of a business incubator or venture fund. I believed too strongly in the entrepreneurial talent of the people who were forced to tread the entrepreneurial path. So strongly that my belief prevented me from taking anti-crisis measures. For instance, we continued renting a whole additional floor in our office building for the needs of a multimedia journalism school, though we could easily have abandoned it and gotten much more money from the savings than we got from the school.

Later on, I admitted my mistake. It would have been right to provide the resources only if they had been abundant and couldn't have been reduced. And even if I had had a burning desire to support startups, it would have been better to choose among the finished projects – ones created by the people who made a conscious choice to become entrepreneurs, and not by my former employees who agreed to try to be entrepreneurs out of despair. Having realized that, I allocated some office space for co-working and started inviting young companies to use our infrastructure. This experience was more successful from a commercial point of view: our sub-lessees allowed us to reduce rental costs and more efficiently use the office units, the costs of which I could not cut further, but which were still not always loaded with work. Communication with the founders of these companies also energized me and gave me the best understanding of what was going on in related industries that interested me. At various times, we housed developers of web services and video games, an HR and branding agency, and other companies. Everybody benefited from it: we supported each other, sometimes ordered services from each other, not to mention the fact that each of us could optimize our expenses.

I think we had one of Russia's first co-working spaces (although we didn't use that term), and I continue to recommend that first-time entrepreneurs choose this option for their first office. Working in the same space with other entrepreneurs, you raise your chances of success.

SUMMARY

Is it advisable to support startups at your company's premises?

1. You can gently suggest that your employees (including former ones whom you know well) set up their own business and use your company's resources the first time. But don't count on profit from these businesses.

2. Provide the resources only if they are really abundant and can't be reduced. For example, if you can't give up some space and save money before the expiration of the rental agreement.

3. You can achieve better results if you invite self-motivated entrepreneurs from outside your company to share your office space and the company's infrastructure.

Chapter 10. Family.

When my current wife Yana and I were just starting to build our life together, before the wedding, she asked me what I was expecting from our relationship. I answered that I was expecting support. I had a reason for that answer: In my first marriage, which broke apart, causing me the deepest suffering, I had an acute lack of support. Yana then confessed to me that she didn't understand what support she could provide, because I had made it quite clear that I wasn't referring to household chores. And I understand her perfectly – I myself couldn't formulate my request clearly. Fortunately for both of us, she agreed to learn, and to her credit, her enthusiasm hasn't died out as the years went by. During the whole of our life together, she has tried to better understand my needs and learn to satisfy them better. Yana came to a point where she became a real specialist in support; she shares her experience in workshops for entrepreneurs' wives, and she even wrote a book, "Moi muzh – predprinimatel" ["My Husband, the Entrepreneur"], which was published by Mann, Ivanov and Ferber in 2014.

I think that the fact that her father was also an entrepreneur, who had to experience not only a breathtaking rise, but ruin, loss of business, and an attempt on his life, played a big role. Therefore, my wife understood in advance that marrying an entrepreneur means high risks and responsibility.

Support, which has been and still is very important to me, is not simply defined. At one moment, I need to be hugged, at another to be listened to, at still another to hear certain words, to see a certain reaction. Naturally, it's more important to feel support at hard times, when belief in your own strength can abandon you, but I believe that people who marry should reach an agreement on mutual support at any moment, irrespective of circumstances. I think it is especially important for the entrepreneur, because lack of support can lead to falling morale, bad business decisions, and, ultimately, jeopardizes the well-being of the whole family. When problems start to emerge in the company, its owner usually watches his employees run away, as they are not ready to sacrifice their earnings and they lose their faith in the employer. At such a moment, the importance of family in the entrepreneur's life increases many times, as other sources of support wane.

I was lucky not only because my wife agreed to support me, but also because we had enough time to learn to support each other before my business entered the next critical period. In the first years of our life together, my business grew, and, in addition to family, there was a community of people who fueled me with energy and enriched me with knowledge. By the way, this is the right approach – don't lay the burden of being the only source of support on a single person, even the one closest to you. As long as you have the opportunity to receive support from different sides, it's just stupid not to take advantage of it. The entrepreneur's responsibility is to provide himself with different forms of support: from mentors, colleagues in business, coaches, etc. – including the family, of course.

Sometime in 2004, I entered a period of self-searching. It seemed to me that I had given enough care to my business to let it continue growing in a semi-automatic mode; my material needs were not badly satisfied, and I started finding myself more often thinking about my real goals and aspirations in life, what I live for and why I do what I do. I spent a lot of time studying and traveling around the world; my wife accompanied me everywhere and shared my desire for self-knowledge. We discussed everything that we learned together, and Yana actually became my personal growth coach – i.e., she provided me that very kind of support that I needed at this period of my life. Constantly enjoying the company of entrepreneurs and speaking on topics related to entrepreneurship, she also conceived a desire to build her own business, and she established a coaching company in 2008. This gave additional value to our relationship. We made the joint discovery that business is an absorbing activity that can be as addicting as a drug, which even competes with the chemistry in a married couple in terms of emotional involvement.

The fact that my wife runs her own business means a lot to me. When I come home from work, I don't have to do what I don't want to do – to become a different person, to forget about work, to set aside all the problems. There is always a person at home who completely shares my values, and yet who has a totally different mindset – a female one – which allows me to see myself from the side and understand myself better.

My wife's entrepreneurial talent allowed me to entrust her with management of the family budget too. At times that were hard for business, when reduction of the company's profits forced me to reduce personal consumption as well, she proved herself to be a good anti-crisis manager too – she immediately reduced family expenses without complaints and lamentations. Seeing that the family treats you not only as a breadwinner, but is ready to share the challenges that befall you – that is also support!

For all that, she doesn't stop bearing children, which for me is the best proof of her belief in me and in our union. Naturally, every couple has their own ideas about how to support each other, and I recommend to entrepreneurs, who have realized the need for more family support to begin with an analysis. What kind of support do you need? When do you feel support from your partner? How can you learn to sense each other's needs better and respond to them? It's important to understand that the support we are discussing in this chapter is not a one-time action, but a lifestyle that implies readiness to always pay attention to one's partner. It's best to form this "support group" not when you, the entrepreneur, are facing betrayal by your business partners and departure of key employees, and suddenly feel an acute need to enlist support from beyond your business circle. In fact, a crisis in the business is the worst time to rebuild family relations. An ideal solution is to agree about everything before marriage, and especially that when choosing a spouse, you make sure that your future wife is able and wants to support her husband, that she is ready to take on responsibilities. I don't believe that support can be spontaneous, unconscious, that it can appear out of the blue. If you are just about to enter into the marriage, observe the relationship between the parents of your bride-to-be: If the father doesn't enjoy the unconditional support of the family, most probably, his daughter has already developed a corresponding attitude toward men. After my first unsuccessful marriage, it was critical for me to marry a woman who would perceive me (and the family) not as an instrument for satisfying her whims, but as a set of contractual obligations (of course the man also assumes responsibilities in the same way).

Naturally, you can build a family without such a deliberate approach, but be prepared for your risks to rise manifold. Unfortunately, divorces are very common in Russia, and as far as entrepreneurs are concerned, the price of a divorce is especially high – both financially and in terms of possible consequences. In my observation, entrepreneurs divorce much more often during economic crises, because latent family conflicts and discontent rise to the surface, stress increases, and without the habit of supporting each other, both partners start to feel badly wounded.

SUMMARY

How can an entrepreneur gain support within the family?

1. Select your wife thoughtfully. Just as no more than 5% of men are able to be entrepreneurs, so no more than 5% of women are suitable to be an entrepreneur's wife.

2. Ideally, your future wife before the marriage (and even before meeting you) should be disposed to support her man, respect him and his mission. Pay attention to how she treats her father and how her mother treats him.

3. Don't hesitate to enter into marriage as into a business deal, where each partner assumes certain obligations. I recommend drawing up a detailed contract in writing – it doesn't have to be official, but it must help the partners realize and accept their obligations to each other.

4. Treat your wife as an investment and not as an object of consumption. Encourage her personal development. A strong, active woman strengthens a marriage.

5. Have children – it affirms the couple's commitment to a long-term relationship.

Chapter 11. Taking care of yourself.

In the third chapter, I mentioned one of the pivotal moments in my life – a trip to a foreign exhibition, which ended in hospitalization and made me review my priorities. Before that, I had been sure that people should work seven days a week. It seemed to me that the entrepreneur should contribute all his energy to the business and strike while the iron is hot. I worked on Saturdays, and expected my employees to do the same. My vacations didn't last for more than one or two days, and while on vacation, I continued thinking about work and worried that something would go wrong in my absence.

When I saw how easily one can undermine one's health even at a young age, I shifted to the other extreme: I started planning 2-3 weeks of vacation, with complete disconnection from work. I cancelled the six-day work week and started getting up without an alarm clock, allowing my body to get as much sleep as it needed. After work, I went to the gym, swam in the swimming pool, and sat in the jacuzzi for as long as I could. Taking care of myself became an inseparable element of my lifestyle: I was worried about my health and tried to stay healthy in every way I knew. Nevertheless, this care was one-sided, in the sense that at work I still wasn't taking care of my health, and my life alternated between relaxation and tension, pleasant and unpleasant things. Now, fifteen years after the crisis, I know there is another way: not to torture oneself at work to the point that you can only return to your senses by total disconnection from anything having to do with work. But I also know that it is easier said than done.

To ease conflicts and tensions at work, I made it my rule to positively welcome all initiatives of employees, partners, and clients, and do so instantaneously, without wasting time thinking them over. You want to do something, I'm all for it, if it's in the best interests of our business. This is when you have to explain, to prove to me that your initiative is in the company's best interests. Because from the very beginning Gameland was an entrepreneurial company, new ideas were generated at different levels of the company almost every day. In the past, the decision-making process sapped my energy and was a constant source of stress; now I have learned to shift some responsibility onto those who generated the ideas.

In the period when I couldn't take care of myself, I felt I was responsible for everyone around me. Who, if not I, will ensure that my employees have a job, that members of my family have financial security and are taken care of? I intentionally ignored the fact that I am a person like everybody else, and I also deserve care; that in addition to obligations, I have the right to a full life.

My deep sense of responsibility revealed itself, for example, in the way I treated negligent employees. If a person didn't do his job well, I could spend years giving him advice and educating him. I remembered that I also didn't understand some things right away, and I figured that the employee was trying to live up to the ideal, but couldn't do it yet. Therefore, I thought, he needs compassion, support, care – and one day he will make it. When I started taking care of myself, I stopped handling those who didn't live up to my expectations with kid gloves. Now I have introduced a "two warnings" rule – if the employee makes the mistake or the error a third time that he was told twice to avoid, it becomes grounds for dismissal.

Another form of my careless attitude toward myself was compromises in selecting my social circle. I devoted a lot of attention to people I didn't enjoy socializing with, either because we were related, or because life had brought us together at some point, or because I found them somewhat useful for my business. Once I decided to take care of myself, I became much more scrupulous about my social connections. I realized that I don't want to poison my life with unpleasant social relations and the equally unpleasant aftertaste that follows them. Once I stopped socializing with unpleasant people, I immediately felt better.

Now I understand that my negligent attitude toward myself at the start of my entrepreneurial career was due to low self-esteem. I didn't appreciate either my time or the effort invested, and didn't realize the value of my contribution to the common goal. On the other hand, I appreciated everything that other people did who worked with me. Many years later, when I started to be regularly invited to speak before entrepreneurs, I learned that many of them, including very successful ones, still haven't gotten used to setting a high value on themselves. Low self-esteem is a constant driver for them, which motivates them to study and to work hard. For example, the founder of a retail chain of a hundred stores doesn't think that he has done anything outstanding: "Big deal! A hundred stores! Walmart has five thousand." The relativity of his success motivates him not to stop at what he has so far achieved. One might think that it is terrific to have such a motivation for development. But in fact, this motivation comes at a price, because the entrepreneur doesn't believe that he himself deserves care; he doesn't take care of himself and neglects his personal interests.

Just several years ago, I managed to find a suitable formula: how to appreciate oneself highly, but not rest on one's laurels, and have the motivation to create. It turned out that it is possible to work a lot, while retaining a high level of energy, enjoying good health and a positive emotional life. The main thing that changed is the concept of rest. Now I don't associate rest with indolence and idleness. If you perceive relaxation as a holiday, it means that all the time that is left (i.e., the time you are working), you are busy doing unpleasant things that are forced upon us. Remember how, in the USSR, they used such concepts as "feat of labor" and "hero of labor"? Does it cross your mind to talk about the heroism of people who enjoy doing what they love? Juxtaposing work and relaxation comes from the times when people couldn't choose work that they love, or were forced to select from a limited range of opportunities; when people were put in prison for "parasitism". When work is such a heavy burden, doing nothing becomes the main luxury, an embodiment of a dream.

When I realized that this schizophrenic concept has nothing to do with me, I started perceiving work as a continuation of myself, and rest as change of activity, which is important in order to look at things from a different perspective, to allow your body, your soul, and your brain to function in a different mode. Education, expansion of the borders of my world, became the highest form of relaxation for me. I like to put myself and my family in an environment where we are either forced to learn, or the atmosphere predisposes us to do so. For instance, we go to another country for a month or two and start learning the local language, learning along the way about daily life at our destination. At the end of the day, we sit and discuss what new and unusual things happened to us that day, what we learned, what conclusions we can draw. It's quite possible that we will change something in our lives from this moment, that we will do some things as they are done by Swedes, Greeks, Frenchmen, Filipinos, or citizens of any other country that we visited – that is if we liked their habits and customs.

Entrepreneurship is a way of life. Openness to new things, a passion to discover the world – it's also a lifestyle that successfully complements how you run your business. Today, making a decision to become an entrepreneur, you aren't necessarily choosing the path that promises the biggest financial gains. It is possible that in Russia, in the 1990s, doing business put you in the community of the country's richest people, but now many government officials and hired managers earn no less and sometimes even more than entrepreneurs, especially considering the fact that the entrepreneur's earnings are often unstable – successful years alternate with the failed ones. For many of us who do business today, wealth has more to do with hope than with reality. So, in my understanding, entrepreneurship is a lifestyle chosen consciously and subconsciously by an individual to enjoy freedom, experience life's unpredictability, and have conditions for continuous development and acquisition of all kinds of experience.

In my observation, the role of the head of a typical enterprise approximates that of the whole rest of the team. Remove the energetic head of a company and replace him with an untalented one, or put employees in conditions where the CEO doesn't assign tasks to them and doesn't require accountability, and productivity will fall by about fifty percent. In crises, the influence of the person in charge of the company's performance becomes even more significant. This is exactly why the entrepreneur's self-care is an investment into an irreplaceable managerial resource which is required for business transformation under the conditions of any crisis, be it fire, "assault" by public officials, rapid changes in the market, etc. Take good care of yourself not because "you deserve it" and not because "you deserve more". There is no need to involve your self-esteem, simply realize the need to replenish the resources of the main source of transformation of your business: yourself.

SUMMARY

Why should an entrepreneur take care of himself? And how do you do it?

1. Realize that the habit of neglecting yourself results from poor self-esteem.

2. Don't play off your work against your personal life; in particular, don't look at your work as a heavy burden, and at relaxation as compensation that you deserve for the torments you have endured. Try to organize your work in such a way as to prevent it from bleeding you dry, even in crisis.

3. Relaxation is a perfect opportunity for education and self-development. The challenge is to think about what and how you should learn to get pleasure from the process.

4. Realize that you can't bear responsibility for everybody's well-being. After all, you are a person, just like everybody else.

5. Don't forget that the CEO is the company's most valuable resource, and, his value rises significantly in a crisis. Don't work yourself into exhaustion, otherwise, you risk losing both your health and your business.

Chapter 12. Sales.

A crisis in a company is usually accompanied by employee drain, not excluding salespeople too, naturally. In this respect, it is very important that each of your clients is the company's client, but not the personal client of a specific salesperson. Among salespeople, there are some who keep clients to themselves. They tell you that they have special, sensitive relations with clients, that everything is based on personal ties and trust. For the client, they invent another fairy-tale to create an illusion of their indispensability. I have had occasions when I didn't manage to make an appointment with a key client for an entire year, because the salesperson who was in contact with him found all kinds of reasons and excuses. Decide in advance whether you want to make your business dependent on such people.

Have you ever heard about brilliant salespeople who can "sell snow to the Inuits?" I have also heard about them, although I have never seen one. In fact, all sales professionals aspire to work with a product that sells itself, that people need. The salesperson can find common language with a client and explain to him the advantages of your offer. And to sell a useless product, one needs a crook's talent, but not the skills of a professional salesperson.

Based on that, I have realized the following concept: if sales go down, at first you should pay attention to the product, and not steal sales "stars" from competitors. In practice, there is not much difference between a "star" and an average (but diligent) salesperson. I made an experiment: I fired a bright sales director and measured the change in revenue of the unit that he headed. The maximum decline was 10%.

I noticed that each salesperson has his own "ceiling," the maximum number of clients, contracts, and money that he is able to generate in a given amount of time. When this ceiling is reached (everyone has his own), further efforts that you might make to motivate your seller and develop his potential, don't bring any results. Having understood that, I started making sure that the working conditions in the sales unit of my company are flexible: each employee has an individual plan, and for some of them, we even introduced a special payment system – a fixed salary, a percentage commission, and bonus parameters, adjusted so as to avoid a situation where each employee, having reached his "ceiling", finds himself regularly compared to more successful colleagues and more is expected of him. In my business, where the product is not typical and standardized, and, therefore it's not a question of massive sales, and the demand fluctuates depending on multiple factors, I oppose a one-size-fits-all policy and long-term contracts that fix obligations of the salesperson and the system of motivation. Instead, I prefer to regularly review the plans, comparing them to the current indicators and making sure that they are still feasible.

There are no ideal salespeople. Different people in this profession have certain skills that are more "upgraded". Some people easily establish contact with a potential client, agree on a meeting. Others are better at conveying the gist of a commercial offer to a client. Closing transactions, collecting the money – that's another talent that doesn't necessarily go along with other skills. If you want to achieve maximum efficiency, it makes sense to identify such "special skills" and entrust different people to deal with the transaction at different stages, taking care to avoid tensions and unnecessary competition between them. What's most important is to remember that you, the entrepreneur, are responsible for the transaction. Shifting this responsibility to a salesperson is the most stupid and irresponsible behavior that can be imagined. A salesperson is but one small (granted, a very important one) link in a long chain of combined efforts that lead to sales; he can't and must not control other links – he won't be able to formulate the idea of a commercial offer for you, he won't select the target audience, and won't conduct marketing research. A large proportion of salespeople are, in fact, "money collectors", who prefer to service already existing demand, not showing any initiative and resourcefulness. Unfortunately, even the so-called "stars" who came to me to apply for a job and provided a solid record of service, demanding a salary of 200,000 rubles, often turned out to be typical "money collectors". Having burned my fingers several times with such people, I started watching closely how they work at the company from their first days. If a person promises to sell 5 million rubles worth of products in a quarter, I don't expect this amount to fall out of the clear blue sky at the end of the quarter – I want to know how many commercial offers were sent out, how many meetings were held, who the prospective clients are, and what the interim results of negotiations are. Based on that, I can estimate the probability of the plan being executed, and, accordingly, understand whether the salesperson deserves his salary. In most cases, such close attention convinces the employee that you and he are not on the same wavelength, that there won't be any easy money here.

Despite multiple failed attempts at hiring experienced salespeople, I still believe that one should keep looking for them. Even if you eliminate 90% of applicants who come from the market, the remaining 10% are worth the effort you invest. But if your business is large enough, you should simultaneously develop your own salespeople – people with no experience, whom you will teach yourself. Try to come to terms in advance with the fact that they won't work with you forever. Very often people who are successful in a sales career, when they reach maturity (after age thirty) feel distressed because of their lack of career growth. It seems to them that appreciation of their contribution should lead to an appointment as sales director or a similar position. However, selling and managing are two radically different functions. A successful salesperson rarely becomes as successful as a manager, and as a result of his promotion, you most probably will lose a good salesperson and get a mediocre manager. And when his failure as sales director becomes evident, there's nothing else left for him but to leave the company and become a salesperson again in a familiar industry (for example, with your chief competitor). If you decide to restrain the career ambitions of your best salesperson, the result may be the same, only this time, the reason for his resignation will be "poor prospects of advancement."

By the way, in order not to feel bitter that your company is performing the role of a foundry producing talent for the market, make employees pay for their training. Novices usually have a lot of energy and motivation, and they haven't yet accumulated an "attitude" and, as a rule, they are ready to earn less in return for experience.

SUMMARY

How to build a sales system which is resistant to crises.

1. Distinguish between salespeople and "money collectors".

2. Remember that you, the entrepreneur, are responsible for the transaction. A salesperson is not a wizard, and he is not the cleverest person in your company with the most initiative. He won't solve problems related to the product, marketing, and a shrinking market.

3. Don't allow your salesperson to become the customer's single point of contact in the company. Maintain personal contacts with key clients.

4. An individual plan and a system of motivation for each salesperson is better than a one-size-fits-all policy.

5. Bring salespeople with different (complementary) talents onto your team and eliminate competition among them.

6. Don't rely only on salespeople from the market: develop your own (at their expense).

7. Note that a successful salesperson seldom becomes a good manager (sales director).

Chapter 13. Education.

When we were developing our own TV channel, I felt my own lack of knowledge in the area of television and arranged training for myself at Fox Channel in the USA. In my meeting with the company's president, I complained that we had invested $5 million dollars in the project, and, in a whole year, the project hadn't become profitable. "You're lucky," he replied. "We invested $400 million and for ten years couldn't make a profit."

When an entrepreneur takes a detached view of a company that is bigger than his own, it seems to him that it employs real professionals, who do everything in an easy and natural way. But if he has a chance for an informal discussion with the people who made the company successful, he would learn to his surprise how many bad decision they were forced to make, what challenges they had to overcome, and how often they found themselves on the brink of collapse.

The reader of this book has surely understood that multiple crises, local and global, were one of my main sources of learning in both business and life. However, that doesn't necessarily mean that I don't recognize other ways of acquiring knowledge. On the contrary, I read a lot, I regularly attend educational conferences for entrepreneurs throughout the world, I hire consultants and coaches, I interview famous entrepreneurs and from each of them I try to learn some useful lessons. Education has a great personal value for me – even greater than financial gains.

"To get MBA or not to get one," is the question that has bothered me throughout my whole entrepreneurial career, and which I continue asking myself to this day. I discussed this question with the deans of the business schools at Harvard, Stanford, MIT Sloan, and Skolkovo. And we mostly came to the conclusion that from the perspective of development of entrepreneurial skills, I would not benefit much from such education. And I don't intend to make career in a corporation.

Actually, it should be noted that almost no one in the world prepares entrepreneurs professionally. Management and entrepreneurship are conceptually different disciplines. And it's simply not a fact that studying management will provide an entrepreneur with the most relevant store of knowledge. I leave open the possibility that the owner of an IT business could be successful in his business with a degree in engineering, without wasting time on studying management theory. I have selected several areas for myself that I study all the time, gaining new knowledge that is really applicable in my business. These are finance, HR, psychology, and case studies of creators of large companies – the latter interest me mostly from the standpoint of how these people make hard decisions and what logic these decisions were based on.

I mentioned above that almost nobody teaches entrepreneurship, and there is a reason for that. An entrepreneur can be taught only by another entrepreneur, a more experienced one; but these people are usually either too busy to share their knowledge, or their time is too expensive, and few can afford to learn from them. I had an opportunity to listen to founders of large companies and talk to them because I am a member of the global Entrepreneurs' Organization (EO). Several times a year, EO conducts business programs oriented at specifically the needs and interests of business owners.

Such an educational format – short and intensive programs – are perfect for me, because I believe in lifelong education. In modern business, it's dangerous to believe that the education you received provides you with an exhaustive store of knowledge: It needs to be replenished and refreshed periodically. I calculated that I spend an average of one month a year on education. This figure doesn't include the time I spend reading business literature.

Entrepreneurship is a special area of activity, where studying someone else's successful experience won't make you more successful. Copying someone's business model, principles of management, marketing strategy, you won't become as great as the entrepreneur who inspired you. To be compared to him, you must follow an unbeaten track, try something revolutionary, risk, fail, and repeat this cycle many times. Nobody will tell you what you need to do. However, someone else's experience can sometimes help you understand what you should not do. Therefore, I always prefer to learn about the mistakes made by other business owners, rather than focusing on what brought them success.

However, the problem is that entrepreneurs are seldom ready to talk about the bad decisions they made, their mistakes and the consequences of such mistakes. First of all, nobody needs it. Modern society has an ingrained culture of honoring the victors, admiring those who achieved something in their life. Mistakes make us ashamed. Journalists and book authors first of all want to draw out the secrets of success from businessmen, as this is what their readers are interested in. Entrepreneurs themselves also prefer to look like heroes in people's eyes, while not acknowledge their weaknesses and failures – after all, it is a kind of self-promotional tool for them. So our opportunities to learn the truth, to arrive at a more or less objective opinion, are significantly limited. The above-mentioned EO is one of the few places where entrepreneurs are encouraged to be as sincere with each other as possible. Another place where successes are always analyzed against the background of mistakes and failures is our magazine Svoy Biznes, which embodies the idea that "only an entrepreneur can teach another entrepreneur".

SUMMARY

What kind of education does an entrepreneur need?

1. Entrepreneurship is not a profession, but a lifestyle. They don't teach that in college.

2. An MBA will hardly turn you into a more successful entrepreneur. Studying at a business school can be postponed until your business grows into a large corporation.

3. An entrepreneur needs applicable knowledge (industry-specific expertise, finance, HR, etc.), but also to develop purely entrepreneurial skills – an ability to choose an unbeaten track, to take significant risks, to turn mistakes into practical experience. This is where communication with other entrepreneurs will come in handy.

4. While studying business cases, an analysis of bad decisions and their consequences will teach you more than a search for the components of success. You don't have many chances to repeat someone else's success, while the chance to avoid someone else's mistakes is quite real.

5. Business is a dynamic game, its rules change all the times, so education should be lifelong.

Chapter 14. Spiritual
and philosophical lessons.

When a non-religious Jew faces sudden challenges, he cries in despair, "What for?" A religious Jew in the same situation will inquire carefully, "What for exactly?" This joke is a fairly accurate illustration of my reaction to crises at different times, at different stages of my spiritual life.

I was raised in a regular Soviet family. Although I am a descendant of an old family of Mountain Jews, it was not customary in our family to remember our roots, to honor our ancestors' traditions, and to take interest in spirituality. I started my independent life as an atheist, and remained one until the crisis of 1998.

Loss of all my money earned in several years of painstaking labor came like a bolt from the blue for me. My world-view didn't account for the fact that the authorities could build a financial pyramid, that the ruble's value would fall by a factor of four, that banks would brazenly steal money from their clients. I had to acknowledge that I simply didn't understand how the world around me worked.

You might remember from first chapters of this book that the 1998 economic crisis in Russia coincided with my personal crisis. My attempt to build a family failed. My health was undermined. On top of everything else, my first child was diagnosed with mental development problems. I had quickly become accustomed to doing well in everything that I started. And then, I got clear evidence that I don't control anything and don't manage anything. It turned out that I am not even in control of my life, my own body. It was a new experience of reality. Probably it was the first time I ever started thinking about who I am and what I live for.

I realized the fact that I was not born of my own volition. Besides, for some reason, I was born in Russia and in a Jewish family. What does it all mean? I had already managed to travel to many countries, I was often in the USA, where my company had an office, and I noticed that people live differently in different places. Why does Russia lag behind the USA in all parameters? Does it mean that we are just like the Americans, only worse? I started looking for answers, reading philosophical books. I was greatly impressed by Lev Gumilev's "Ethnogenesis and the Biosphere," which directed my attention for the first time to the existence of philosophical laws of the universe.

Probably, the universe is too complex a concept for our understanding, but we can study its laws and try to understand what is within our power. Studying philosophical works, I gradually came to understand that there must exist a powerful force in the world, which established the higher laws. At the same time, looking for the answer to the question "Whom am I?" I started wondering how Jews differ from other people. And I learned that for a Jew, the most important thing is to keep the commandments.

In the commandments of Judaism, I saw a means of harmonious existence in a complex world. Now I am thankful to that crisis for pushing me out of my comfort zone, allowing me to look at the world from a different angle, and forcing me to study. We study more actively and willingly when we have problems. In satiety and comfort, we simply have no motivation to acquire new knowledge: the mind thinks that we are doing great, and we should keep doing what we are doing. Looking back, I see that the richest periods of my life actually coincided with crises.

During my first serious crisis, I didn't understand why all these challenges befell me; they seemed completely unjust, undeserved, and out of all proportion. Today, I laugh at that view of those events; I see them as completely natural, even without any spiritual undertones, within the frameworks of the material world. For example, knowledge of how an economy works and the public availability of basic data allow us to forecast an economic crisis in the country. For this reason, the 2008 crisis was no surprise to me, and I started warning everybody about the 2014 crisis a year and a half in advance.

I don't claim that everything in the world has become clear and predictable for me. I have simply realized that all phenomena in the world, regardless of how harsh, absurd, and unjust they might seem to us, are, in fact, logical and can be explained. I can't explain many phenomena, but I'd rather try to get to the bottom of such things than to deny their existence from the perspective of my own illiteracy. It has never occurred to me to consider myself a victim of bad circumstances or an imperfect world.

Even the most tragic events in human life, such as the death of family members, are perceived differently from a spiritual perspective. You try to understand what role you are assigned to play in this event. And you don't think that something that rightfully belonged to you was taken away from you. There is always an animal element in human nature, which reacts to negative events with indignation and hopelessness. But when we discover a spiritual element in ourselves, we more often ask ourselves why this or that event happens to us, never doubting that it was supposed to happen.

Of the recent years, 2013 was the hardest one for me, when the company's sales dropped dramatically, most publishing projects became unprofitable, and key employees assumed obligations that they couldn't fulfill. The height of this hard year was my conflict with the former editor of Digital Photo magazine Boris Muradov, who publicly accused me of tampering with the management accounting that allegedly resulted in his claim that a profitable project, headed by him, turned into an unprofitable one. In other words, it was an accusation of theft from my own colleagues. When all the arguments in this discussion were exhausted, I demanded that my opponent leave the office. He didn't obey, and I couldn't refrain from the use of physical force: I pushed him out. After that, Muradov filed a police statement, and I became involved in a criminal case and was sentenced. When all these events were happening to me, I tried to understand their meaning, what I had to learn from them. Why did I use force? After all, I don't need to be told that intelligent people don't sort things out that way.

Analyzing the reasons that made me lose self-control, I came to a conclusion that I am too dependent on what other people think: if people say bad things about me, accuse me of sins I have not committed, I am overwhelmed with a sense of injustice and offense. But why does it happen? After all, I wrote just above that in my view of the world, nothing happens that is unjust. Unfortunately, simply realizing this truth is not enough; it needs to be accepted on a deeper level, the level of spontaneous reactions. Simply said, even if you know something, that doesn't mean you can act upon it. That was the idea that I took from my lesson.

The beauty of the spiritual growth is that it doesn't have a highest point, where you can relax and say that you have achieved everything. It is an endless path: no matter how many new things you learn, what level of development you achieve, life will always point you at your imperfection and will suggest how you should develop further.

I will note that my aspiration to lead a spiritual life has never contradicted the material world. Having accepted a religious world view, I still love to live life to the fullest. Spirituality attracts me as a theoretical discipline, and the last thing I want is to turn into a learned religious scholar or a philosopher. I treasure all the discoveries that I made on my way to spiritual development, because they have a practical application. Doing business gives me an opportunity to apply my knowledge in practice. An analogy: everybody knows that jogging is good for your health, but who really jogs? In this respect, business provides incredible opportunities for the self-realization of a searching person.

SUMMARY

A spiritual perspective on challenges

1. A crisis is an educational situation, not a punishment.

2. Accept the fact that any crisis is a natural and lawful event, even if it completely caught you off guard. Your goal is to recognize these lawful patterns.

3. Don't say, "It shouldn't have happened." Better ask, "What is my role in this event?"

4. Knowledge and skill are different things. Don't restrict yourself to knowledge; sharpen your practical skills.

5. One's own business offers a unique opportunity to put the laws of the universe to practice.

6. Development is infinite. Perfection is unattainable.

www.ingramcontent.com/pod-product-compliance
Lightning Source LLC
Chambersburg PA
CBHW070926220526
45468CB00005B/1681